Looking After Your ·DOG·

Looking After Your
·DOG·

· Edited by Ian Kearey ·

PARRAGON

First published in Great Britain in 1997 by
Parragon
Unit 13–17
Avonbridge Trading Estate
Atlantic Road
Avonmouth
Bristol BS11 9QD

ISBN: 0-7525-2160-8

Produced by Haldane Mason, London.

Acknowledgements
Art Director: **Ron Samuels**
Design: **Digital Artworks Partnership Ltd**
Illustration: **Robert Farnworth**
Picture Research: **Charles Dixon-Spain**

Printed in Italy

Picture Acknowledgements
All photographs by **Animals Unlimited**

Material in this book has previously appeared
in *The Complete Book of Dog Care* by Jane Oliver

• CONTENTS •

Introduction

Once a dog joins your household it will be part of
the family for the next 15 years or more, so it is
important to consider what you and the dog need from
one another. You may want a companion, a protector and
a playmate for the children, or you may have ambitions
for a dog as a competitor in obedience trials
or the show ring.

Your reasons for wanting a dog as a pet will make
a considerable difference to the type of dog you choose,
but whether the dog you select is large or small, pedigree or
mongrel, dignified or sporting, it will demand a great deal from
you in terms of time, attention and care. Cuddly puppies can
grow up into energetic, hungry and wilful adults, so before
you take the plunge, make certain that you have room for
a dog in your life, and remember that a dog's loyalty and
devotion will repay all the time and money you
spend many times over.

Chapter 1

A New Dog

*D*ogs come in all shapes and sizes, and it is essential to choose a shape and size that suits your home and lifestyle.

First, consider the size and type of your home. It would be unkind to confine a Great Dane or an Irish Wolfhound to a small flat; they need plenty of living space. If you live at the top of three flights of stairs, remember that you might have to carry down a sick or convalescent animal two or three times a day for toilet requirements. Then think about where and how you will exercise your dog. If the only available exercise is round a city block, then a Retriever, Setter or Greyhound would be an unsuitable choice, however much you admire

Whether a pedigree Afghan or a 57-varieties mongrel, dogs are devoted companions.

their looks. Consider how much time you can devote to training a dog; if your life is too busy to allow the time necessary, you should not take on strong, potentially fierce dogs that need firm handling and careful training.

Last but not least, think about the cost: a large dog will be considerably more expensive than a small one.

• *A new dog quickly becomes one of the family.*

DOG COSTS

Over its lifetime, your dog will cost you some thousands of pounds, so it is wise to estimate for the essentials in advance. Take into account:

- Initial outlay: bed, indoor or outdoor kennel, food bowls, toys, collar and lead.

- Food: the larger the dog, the bigger the food bill.

- Neutering: more expensive for females than males.

- Vaccinations and annual boosters.

- Veterinary bills for illness: an unknown quantity.

- Professional clipping and grooming.

- Training and obedience classes.

- Extra fencing needed to keep your dog on your property: this must always be well maintained.

- Damage replacement: puppies or destructive adult dogs can add quite a bit to household costs.

Examining a puppy

• The eyes should be bright and clear, with no discharge and no sign of inflammation. The ears should be clean inside with no sign of discharge, and odour-free. The hairs around the edge should be clean. Also, notice if the puppy scratches at any part of his body, especially his ears, as this can be a sign of infection, or an indication that the coat is infested with fleas. •

TYPES OF DOG

Even if you have a good idea of the dog you want, take the trouble to read one of the many books outlining the characteristics and temperament of each breed, in case there is something you have overlooked. You can see the various breeds going through their paces at dog shows, and most owners will be only too pleased to tell you all about their favoured breed.

GOOD LOYAL COMPANIONS: Affenpinscher, Border Terrier, Boxer, Collie, Dachshund, English Terrier, Fox Terrier, Irish Terrier, Irish Wolfhound, King Charles Spaniel, Pug

GOOD WITH CHILDREN: Basenji, Border Terrier, Boxer, Bull Terrier, English Setter, Labrador Retriever, Staffordshire Bull Terrier, Siberian Husky

GOOD GUARDS: Bouvier des Flandres, Bullmastiff, Dalmatian, Dobermann, German Shepherd, Great Dane, Old English Sheepdog, Rottweiler, Schipperke, Welsh Corgi

GOOD FOR TRAINING: Australian Cattle Dog, Border Collie, Dobermann, German Shepherd, Golden Retriever, Labrador, Poodle, Schnauze, Weimaraner

Examining a puppy

• The body should have a moderate layer of fat under the skin, and the skin should be loose and pliable. If the ribs feel bony but the skin is stretched tight over the abdomen, the puppy may have worms. If this is the case, then check the puppy's vaccination record for other irregularities. •

Essential equipment

The puppy's first bed can be a cardboard box lined with newspaper and old sweaters. Beanbags filled with polystyrene granules, with washable outer covers, provide a cosy nest, plastic beds lined with washable mattresses are durable and chew-proof, and small dogs can cuddle into an 'igloo' bed. Wicker beds are good for chewing, but pieces could be swallowed. Any bed should be big enough to allow the dog to stretch out and to turn round and round before settling down.

Breeds with long, pendulous ears need a food bowl with fairly tall sides that slope inwards at the top. Stainless steel bowls with a rubber rim underneath are easy to keep clean and well worth the extra cost. Use a heavy pottery bowl for water. Keep a special knife and fork, and wash all utensils used for dogs separately from family dishes.

A leather leash will need oiling to keep it in good condition. Nylon leashes are cheaper, easy to wash and fold into your pocket, but are not suitable for a large, heavy dog. Extending leashes give a dog more freedom, while still leaving the owner in control.

PUPPY TIPS

- With a new puppy in the house, keep outside doors locked and windows closed.

Healthy puppies are always interested in what you are doing.

- Keep breakables out of reach, and unplug electrical items in case the puppy chews the flex.

- Keep the puppy indoors until it is fully protected by vaccination.

- Don't smack your puppy if it makes mistakes; it will probably be thoroughly bewildered and it may come to fear you.

- Make sure your puppy has plenty of company; it should not be left alone for long periods or shut away from the rest of the family.

A long walk in the countryside is good for both dogs and owners.

The first days

Arrange to collect your dog when there will be someone at home most of the day for at least the first week.

Collect the puppy by car if possible, and have a cardboard box lined with a blanket in the back. If you have to travel by public transport, use a secure carrier that can be thoroughly washed afterwards. Line a cardboard carrying case with a plastic sheet and plenty of newspaper and support it underneath, not just by the handle.

At home, take the puppy outside and stay with it there for a few minutes. If it performs, praise it effusively. Then take it indoors and keep it in one room for the time being. Stay with it; a new puppy will become very distressed if it is shut away alone. Shortly after arrival, offer a small meal. Once it has eaten, take it outside again. Then let it sleep.

Let your puppy meet the rest of the family one at a time, in peaceful surroundings. Children must understand that squeezing, teasing and pulling are not allowed and that after half an hour of play, a puppy needs to sleep.

Housetraining with paper

• Confine the puppy to one easily cleaned room, preferably with an outside door, and cover the floor with several layers of newspaper. The puppy will probably pick one area and return to it. Once this happens, remove the paper from the rest of the floor, leaving a single toilet area. Move this gradually towards the door, then leave the door open and place the newspaper outside. Once the routine is well-established, dispense with the paper. •

Chapter 2

Food and Feeding

There is no difficulty about providing a balanced diet for your dog; there are plenty of good proprietary foods on the market and, properly used, they will keep your dog in peak condition.

The main problem for most owners is limiting diet to a healthy amount.

In the wild, dogs will gorge themselves whenever food is available, eating all they can get because they do not know when their next meal is coming; many domestic dogs, even though regularly and well fed, will behave in the same way.

Children and puppies often form a life-long bond.

They also became experts at wheedling tidbits and table scraps from their owners at every opportunity, and this can lead to obesity and many attendant problems.

• *A healthy, well-nourished dog is a pleasure to see and own.*

Puppies

When you bring your puppy home, keep to its accustomed diet for the time being. Any changes should be phased in little by little. The golden rule for feeding puppies is little and often.

Until four months, puppies should have four meals a day, the first and third meal usually being baby cereal or puppy meal soaked in milk, and the second and fourth being canned puppy food or mince mixed with bread or puppy biscuits. If your puppy looks rather lean, add more cereal and biscuits, but if it is looking podgy, cut down on the carbohydrates.

After four months, cut out the first meal and increase the quantity of food at other meals. At six or seven months, cut out the other milk and cereal meal, and from about nine months you can feed a single meal a day.

Puppies tend to chew anything that comes their way, so they ingest all sorts of rubbish, and normally they seem to come to no harm. Occasional slight diarrhoea is nothing to worry about, but if it persists and the puppy seems bright and healthy otherwise, try cutting the amount of milk in the diet.

FEEDING DO'S & DONT'S

- Do make sure that clean water is always available.

- Don't feed your dog on cat food; its protein content is too high.

Dogs love swimming and are always fascinated by water.

- Do serve food at room temperature, not straight from the refrigerator.

- Don't expect your dog to live on table scraps; our food is highly processed and will not contain all the necessary nutrients.

- Do add a little vegetable oil to the feed if your dog's coat is looking dull.

- Don't overfeed your dog; obesity will probably shorten its life.

Collies are noted for their quickness and intelligence.

Types of food

Some canned foods provide a 'complete' food, with cereal already added, while others need added meal. Dogs who will not eat meat mixed with meal can be given biscuits instead, either with the meat or as tidbits, but be careful to ration them, so that you are not giving extra carbohydrate treats all day long.

Semi-moist food comes in foil sachets, each with an average serving, which can be stored without refrigeration before opening. Semi-moist food is relatively expensive but can be useful for fussy feeders, though it is unsuitable for diabetic dogs.

Usually in the form of flakes or pellets, dried food is a relatively low-cost way of feeding your dog, and it will not spoil. It can be stored for some weeks but will eventually lose its vitamin content, so keep an eye on the 'use by' date on the packet.

If you feed your dog on home cooking, provide a good mix of meat with vegetables, some white fish and poultry as well as bread, rice and cereals. Feed offal only once or twice a week. All meat and fish should be cooked.

• *While still very young, puppies begin to assert themselves at feeding times. Although a natural consequence of large litters, this may cause problems, as the pushy puppies can end up overweight and suffer ill-health as a result. The less assertive ones sometimes get less than their share, and it is difficult to tell whether the puppy is underweight because it is not eating enough, or if it is unwell. As they get older, therefore, it is a good idea to feed puppies from individual bowls.*

Fussy and greedy dogs

If your dog is picky, cut out all between-meal snacks. Feed your dog one or two meals a day and cut down on the amount of fibre.

Miniature and toy breeds have all the qualities of larger dogs.

Toy breeds are very good at manipulating their owners, rejecting canned dog food because they know that something better will be offered. The only answer is to be firm: put down the dish and leave it for, at most, an hour, then take it up again. Offer the same type of food at the next meal and follow the same procedure.

Fat dogs are not healthy dogs: obesity leads to heart disease, arthritis and diabetes, and brings added risks if the dog needs an anaesthetic for surgery. Ideally, you should be able to feel, but not see, the dog's ribs. If you can see its sides bulging as it faces you head-on, then it is too fat. Feed several small meals instead of one large one, and plan activities to involve and interest the dog before and after mealtimes. Add bran to the food to help it feel full.

Bones

• Bones are not essential for a dog's wellbeing and, though on the whole they are good for teeth, helping to keep them clean, they can sometimes cause teeth to fracture. Never give poultry bones, as these splinter and can become stuck in the mouth or throat. Large knuckle bones are the safest type, and even these should not be cooked, as this hardens them so that they are more likely to damage teeth. •

Chapter 3

Training Your Dog

*D*ogs enjoy order and structure in their lives, and a well-trained dog is a happy and contented dog.

The dog knows what is expected of it and the owner is relaxed and in control, which produces an all-round feeling of security and confidence.

Basic dog training is not difficult, but it does demand a fair degree of commitment on the part of the owner.

Dogs have a huge variety of appealing facial expressions.

Half-hearted training, with the owner giving up whenever patience and persistence is required, is useless and will only leave the dog bewildered and undisciplined.

Whether you want a well-mannered pet or a dog capable of winning obedience trials, the earlier you begin, the better.

• *All dogs enjoy learning tricks and respond well to training.*

Rewards

Food rewards can play a crucial role in training. In the wild, much of the dog's waking time would be spent finding food, and this instinct still runs deep. When you plan a training session, take a little packet of tidbits along. Whenever the dog hears the bag rustle, it will know that it can be rewarded when it has obeyed a command. Once you have practised a command successfully several times, continue to reinforce the behaviour intermittently, giving a tidbit every fourth or sixth time the dog obeys. Soon the dog will respond without the promise of food.

Teaching a dog to alter its behaviour because it wants to is more effective than punitive methods. When your dog has done what is required, be generous with praise, give your dog a good rub or whatever it likes best, and it will want to do the same thing again to get the same result. You can often check unwanted behaviour successfully by withholding attention. Turn away from the dog, and don't look at it or speak to it. A few minutes will be enough; dogs hate to be ignored, and they soon get the message.

TRAINING TIPS

- Be firm, patient and kind.

- A single member of the family, preferably the 'pack leader', should undertake the early training.

- Vary the exercises in every training session.

- Avoid battles of will; distract the dog's attention before you reach deadlock.

- Use a long training leash for all early training out of doors.

- Be prepared to repeat the same exercise several times every day.

- Don't move on to the next stage too quickly; make sure that every step has been thoroughly mastered before tackling a new task.

- Decide which word you will use for each command and stick to it, otherwise the dog will become confused.

- Remember that success breeds success. Finish off an unsatisfactory session with a familiar exercise so that the dog can succeed and be praised.

- Keep the sessions short; never persist until the dog is bored.

'COME' TRAINING

This is an exercise you can practise indoors with your dog or puppy.

Wait until your dog is looking at you from the other side of the room then, when it begins to move towards you, say 'Come!' and, stooping slightly, extend both arms forwards and slightly sideways in a welcoming gesture. Bend down to the dog's level and give it an enjoyable rub, telling it how well it has done.

Good training is partly a matter of patiently gaining a dog's interest.

Use this technique frequently, so that the puppy gets to know the word and the gesture.

When you are ready to begin training outside, let the dog trot beside you on the leash, then call its name, say 'Come!' and start walking backwards, giving a gentle pull on the leash if necessary. The dog will come to look on this as a game, and it should respond easily.

Pulling the leash

• If you need to pull the leash to make the dog come, always pull gently. Use your voice to beckon your dog and never get into a pulling contest, as this will only make things worse •

'SIT' TRAINING

This exercise makes use of the dog's natural responses.

At meal-times, hold the dog's food bowl over its head and say 'Sit!' firmly, with an emphasis on the 't'. If you back the dog so that its rump is near the wall it will probably sit instinctively, but if it does not get the idea, put your other hand on its rump and press gently. Insist that it sits properly, rather than half-squatting, wait a couple of seconds, then praise it and put down the food.

When the meal-time lesson has been learned, practise outside, holding your hand above the dog's head and giving the same command. The first time, have a tidbit in your hand, but after that only give the dog a tidbit occasionally. Eventually you can abandon the food rewards altogether.

Decide on a release word that can be used whenever an exercise is completed, so that the dog knows it can get up and move off. Your dog will not understand the word itself, only its associations, but don't choose a word that sounds too much like any of the other commands you plan to give.

• *If you feel, for whatever reason, that you need help in training your dog or puppy, you will probably be able to find a local dog-training class. Most of these take dogs from six months old, and an introductory course will teach basic exercises and offer tips on solving behavioural problems: a course usually lasts about eight or nine weeks. However, don't make the mistake of thinking that all you will have to do is turn up for each class every week, and that will train your dog. It is essential that you practise the techniques you learn and reinforce your dog's lessons every day, otherwise your time and money will have been wasted.*

'HEEL' TRAINING

This exercise can be done both as a lesson and on a walk.

When training your dog to walk to heel, always keep the dog on the same side. Most trainers keep the dog on the left and carry the leash in the right hand, and you can hold a favourite toy or a bag containing a few tidbits in your left hand. As you step off, say 'Heel!' and give a hand signal, sweeping your left hand forward in front of the dog's nose. Walk

A dog will always enjoy pleasing its owner or trainer.

your dog briskly and keep its attention by tapping your leg or chatting companionably. Make lots of right turns, and occasionally give a tidbit when the dog has its shoulder alongside your left knee. If it pulls forward (most dogs want to walk faster than their owners and to lead the way), give a quick tug on the leash and say 'Heel!' firmly. Don't try to haul your dog backwards, or you may end up in a tug-of-war. If the dog keeps pulling to the left, walk close to a fence or wall. The sessions should not be too long; alternate two or three heeling routines with other exercises to keep the dog's interest.

Tapping your leg

• *Tapping your leg should be a sign of encouragement for your dog; be consistent with this. As long as he is talked to or acknowledged at every stage of his learning process you will find him always attentive and always happy to be with you.*•

'FETCH' TRAINING

Use your dog's natural instinct for chasing a moving object to teach retrieving. Begin with your dog at your left-hand side on a long leash and throw a favourite toy a few paces in front. Choose something that will bounce or

Well-cared for and loved dogs are alert and quick to please.

tumble to attract the dog's interest then, as soon as the dog moves to chase the toy, say 'Fetch!'. Once the dog has picked up the toy, let it run about with it for a couple of minutes while you keep the leash slack. Then call 'Come!' and if necessary, pull the leash gently. When the dog returns, have it sit in front of you, and offer a tidbit in exchange for the toy. As the dog drops the toy, say 'Give!' or 'Drop!', then give plenty of praise. If the dog drops the toy voluntarily when it returns to you, you should still give the command and the tidbit. As with the other exercises, phase out the tidbits. Increase the distance you throw the toy little by little then, once the dog is obeying commands well, try the exercise off the leash in a safe area.

Ready to fetch

• As with all training, keep your dog by your side before giving a command. Make sure you congratulate your dog thoroughly in the early stages, and make sure he or she knows this can be a game too. Balls, toys and sticks all make good things to fetch. •

Chapter 4

Caring for Your Dog

*T*aking care of your dog means understanding its needs and natural instincts, and being firm as well as affectionate.

A well-cared-for dog is a balanced dog. However humans may have modified dogs in their various breeds, they are all descended from a wild ancestor, the wolf.

Though our domestic dogs do not have to hunt for food or protect themselves and their offspring from predators, they retain their hunting and protective instincts, coupled with the keen senses that would have enabled them to survive in the wild.

Be prepared to give working dogs a lot of exercise.

At the same time, dogs need from their owners the companionship and stimulus that their ancestors got from the pack, and a knowledge and awareness of your dog's physical and mental requirements will pay dividends for both of you.

• *Long-haired dogs require regular and thorough grooming.*

Body language

An alert dog will have its tail and head up and its ears pricked (according to breed), and if its tail is wagging and its movements are bouncy, it's pretty pleased with life.

A fearful dog will cringe low, with its ears flattened and its tail tucked between its legs.

An aggressive dog will stand with head and tail held high, making itself look as large as possible to create maximum impact. Once the hackles rise along the back and shoulders and the lips curl back to show plenty of teeth, it is thinking about attacking.

A submissive dog will roll over on its back, with its belly exposed and one leg slightly raised.

A playful dog will begin with a 'play-bow', dropping down on its forelimbs with its rump raised in the air, keeping eye contact with the intended playmate. This will usually be followed by a good deal of bouncing around and tail-wagging to encourage the playmate to join in a game. Between two dogs, this usually results in an excited chase and a mock fight.

• *A happy dog will show endless affection to its owner.*

PLAY

Play is essential to your puppy's development, and dogs continue to play throughout their lives. Playing games gives an outlet for natural canine behaviour.

- Balls should not be smaller than tennis balls for medium-sized dogs; for a larger dog, use a bigger size to stop a ball lodging in the throat.
- Squeaky toys should be made of latex. Take care, however, as dogs have been known to 'attack' a child, attracted by a squeaky toy.
- Nylon chews help keep the teeth and gums healthy, but not all dogs enjoy gnawing at them indefinitely.
- Dumbbells are ideal for retrieving games.
- Kongs are made of chew-resistant rubber which bounces in an unpredictable way.
- Frisbees are good toys, but only use those made of light material as they could otherwise cause damage to the dog's mouth and teeth when it catches one.
- Dogs always enjoy a tug-of-war with tug toys, and can play happily with another dog. A knotted rope makes a good alternative. Do not play tugging games with very assertive dogs. Some dogs enjoy swinging on anything hanging from a tree, and small and medium-sized animals will ride inside a swinging car tyre.

• *Dogs enjoy being outdoors, whatever the weather or temperature.*

Grooming

Long-haired dogs will need daily grooming; it is unwise to skip it for several days only to find that you have to deal with matted lumps, which will hurt the dog and cause it to resist grooming in the future. Short-haired breeds need less attention, but regular grooming is important for every type of dog. It massages the skin, stimulates the circulation and improves general condition; it removes tangles and any foreign bodies stuck in the hair; and it removes dead hair which will otherwise be shed over your furniture.

During grooming your dog should be at a height comfortable for you: small dogs can be groomed on your lap, but for larger breeds it will be more convenient to stand the dog on an old table. Each breed has its own requirements, and the equipment you will need may vary. A smooth-haired dog can be groomed with a body brush, while others will need a bristle brush to do the job satisfactorily. A carder (rectangular board with wire teeth) is ideal for dealing with the undercoat of short-haired dogs, while a rubber grooming mitten will remove dead hair from the outer coat.

Grooming with a brush

• Hold up the dog's head, brush down the throat and between the forelegs. Brush the fine hair of the stomach with firm but gentle strokes, right from the roots, paying special attention to any bits of twig or grass seeds that might be caught in the coat. •

Bathing

Dogs should not be bathed more often than absolutely necessary, as it removes natural oils from the coat and may leave it looking dull. However, some dogs love to roll in anything smelly. You will need canine shampoo, a jug, several towels and, for a small dog, a plastic bowl or an old baby bath. A larger dog can stand in a bathtub or on a concrete patio near a drain outlet. Wear a plastic apron.

Plug the dog's ears with cotton wool and stand it in a little warm water. Pour warm water over the coat, starting at the hindquarters and working forwards. Use the shampoo to work up a lather, massaging against the lie of the coat. Make sure the underside and the legs are washed thoroughly.

With a little shampoo on your fingertips, lather the head gently, keeping shampoo away from the eyes and the mouth.

Rinse and dry the head, and rinse the rest of the body with warm water. Squeeze as much excess water as possible from the coat and legs. Lift the dog out of the bath and wrap it in a towel, rubbing vigorously. Long coats should be groomed into place while drying.

Dry shampoo

• Give the coat a final polish with a chamois leather kept specially for the purpose. If your dog has a light-coloured coat, it may benefit from dry shampooing. This is no substitute for a bath but it can remove grease and make the coat look cleaner, thus avoiding excessive washing, which can be detrimental to the coat. The powder is sprinkled on, left a short time, then brushed out thoroughly. •

Chapter 5

Behaviour

*E*very time your dog settles down in your best armchair or launches itself in delight at a visiting neighbour, it is establishing a habit, and the longer the habit is allowed to persist, the more time and effort it will take you to put things right.

It may be amusing when your excited puppy strains at the leash or begs a biscuit from your plate, but it is not nearly so funny when your full-grown dog drags you round the park or steals your guest's sandwich from under his nose.

Bad behaviour needs to be tackled with firmness and consistency. Always correct, rather than punish, the dog.

Every breed has its devotees, and will repay affection and discipline.

Punishment is pointless unless administered at the moment of misbehaviour; just a few seconds later, the dog has no idea why you are being unkind.

• *Cuddles are an important part of the relationship between dog and owner.*

Jumping and barking

You may not mind your dog leaping to greet you, but your visitors certainly will. If the dog is large, try bringing up your knee into the dog's chest each time it tries to jump up. Alternatively, catch hold of the dog's paws, one in each hand. Don't speak to your dog, but look over its head and hold out its paws, without squeezing, until it is struggling to get away. When all four paws are firmly on the floor, bend down to the dog's level to greet and pet it.

In a good home, any dog will feel secure and contented.

Most owners welcome barking that warns off intruders – but not for 20 minutes every time the doorbell rings. You will need the help of a friend who will walk briskly up to the door then, once the barking starts, retreat quietly. Allow the dog half a dozen barks, then distract its attention: some trainers bang a metal tray on a table, crash two baking tins together or use a water pistol. When it stops barking, give a tidbit and plenty of praise. Repeat the process. Eventually, lengthen the time between the end of barking and giving the tidbit, so that the dog remains quiet for several seconds before getting the reward.

Making friends

• A dog that treats welcome visitors like burglars, barking incessantly or baring its teeth in a growl as they step inside, is not an asset to any home. If it is unreliable, bring your dog in on a leash to greet a new visitor. At any sign of aggression from the dog, give a sudden jerk on the leash – not to haul the dog towards you, but to win its attention. Once the dog is calm, the visitor can approach quietly. •

DO'S AND DONT'S FOR IMPROVING BEHAVIOUR

• Do look at the problem from the dog's point of view: this could well explain why it is happening.

• Don't hit a 'bad' dog under any circumstances, and don't lose your temper; use your tone of voice to indicate displeasure.

Mongrels are among the sparkiest and most lively of dogs.

• Do remember that prevention is better than cure; avoid situations which prompt problem behaviour.

• Don't leave your dog to its own devices for so long that it becomes bored or badly behaved.

• Do give plenty of praise when your dog responds to correction or switches attention from unwanted behaviour.

Aggression

This is the most serious canine behaviour problem, as it can lead to actual bodily harm, and could mean a death sentence for your dog. Stem any aggressive tendencies as soon as they show themselves; a puppy should never get away with growling when a toy is taken away or when a visitor walks into the house. Never let your dog get the upper hand in the household.

When you are walking outdoors, where you meet and pass other dogs, your normally peaceful dog may become over-protective or jealous about other dogs coming near you, and attempt to drive other animals away. A dog prone to chasing and fighting should always be on a leash outside its own garden, and when you pass another dog, make sure that your body is between the two animals.

If your dog shows too much interest in a potential adversary, use its name, jerk the leash, then turn round sharply, so that your dog finds itself quickly walking away from its enemy. Keep talking to your dog, and praise it for doing well.

Chapter 6

Health Care

Your dog cannot talk and tell you when it is ill or in pain, so your best guide to your pet's health is your own observation.

Dogs are creatures of habit and, though the odd 'not-too-well' day may mean nothing, if they act in an uncharacteristic manner for longer than that, they may need a veterinary checkup.

Using the dog's nose as the barometer of health is very unwise – many a healthy dog may have a dry nose, while the nose of a sickly animal may remain wet. A more reliable guide is your dog's general behaviour: if it is listless, irritable and indifferent when you suggest a game or a walk, there may be a problem.

Alert, bright-eyed and eager – the signs of a healthy dog.

If it is frightened or in pain, your normally docile and affectionate dog may turn on you and possibly injure you. In this situation, wear a pair of gloves or have a blanket or coat to hand, to wrap round the dog.

• Being with your dog helps it when it is ill or at the vet.

CHECKING YOUR DOG'S HEALTH

If your dog shows any of the following symptoms, you should take it to the veterinarian immediately (if you go away on holiday, ensure that your carer has this list).

- Excessive thirst

- Eating little or nothing for more than 24 hours

- Bleeding from the mouth, nose, anus or genitals

- Straining to pass urine

- Generally dull or lethargic appearance

- Noticeable weight loss (you can check the dog's weight by weighing yourself, then picking up the dog and comparing the two weights)

- Lameness, difficulty in movement or over-sensitivity when touched

Always be aware of indications that your dog may not be well.

FIRST-AID KIT

Some minor injuries, such as flesh wounds or even choking, can be treated by the owner, but the golden rule is to consult a veterinarian as soon as the immediate danger is passed. If you are in any doubt about the dog's condition, ring the veterinary surgery right away and outline the symptoms clearly; the staff will advise you on whether an early appointment is necessary. Keep a first aid kit of the following things:

Regular visits to the vet are part of a dog's routine.

• Thermometer

• Blunt-ended scissors

• Tweezers

• Gauze pads

• Cotton wool and buds

• Bandages

• Petroleum jelly

• Antiseptic cream, as recommended by your vet

Choosing a vet

When choosing a veterinarian, ask local dog owners or dog breeders to find the most highly-rated practitioner in the area. When you first acquire your dog, take it along for a check-up, whether it needs vaccinations or not. The veterinarian will then know your dog and have a record of its past history. Check whether he or she is willing to make housecalls if necessary, and what arrangements are made for 24-hour emergency cover.

When you take your dog along for treatment, make a note of any symptoms and how long they have lasted so far. Be precise about any change in eating, drinking or toilet habits, any change in the appearance of faeces, or any alterations in behaviour. The more details the veterinarian has to work on, the more accurate the diagnosis is likely to be.

If you want to change your veterinarian, either because you move house or because you are not satisfied with the service you get, it is in your dog's interest to notify your current practice. You do not need to give any explanation; simply ask for your dog's records to be transferred to your new veterinarian.

Taking a temperature

• A dog's normal temperature varies between 38° and 39°C (100° and 102°F), and it can be useful to check this if you are wondering if a veterinary appointment is necessary. Use a snub-nosed glass thermometer, the end greased with vegetable oil. Shake the mercury, then lift the dog's tail and insert the thermometer slowly for about 2.5 cm (1 in) into the dog's rectum. Hold it for about half a minute, then remove and wipe clean before reading the dog's temperature. •

Nursing a sick dog

The bed should be in a quiet, warm, well-ventilated place without draughts. A well-wrapped hot water bottle filled with warm water will help to keep it snug. Layers of newspaper topped with old towels or sweaters will make comfortable bedding which can be changed as required.

If the dog is off its food, tempt it with small, frequent meals of cooked white fish or poultry or scrambled egg. Warm the food to blood temperature, and feed by hand if necessary. Dehydration can be a danger, particularly if the dog is vomiting or has diarrhoea. While the dog is ill, clean its face regularly by wiping away any discharge from around the eyes, nose and mouth, using a clean pad of dampened cotton wool for each area. If it suffers from diarrhoea, you will need to clean its rear end as well.

When the dog needs to go outside, take it out for the shortest possible time. If it is too ill to walk, carry it out wrapped in a blanket and put it down in the appropriate place. Alternatively, use plenty of newspaper in one corner of a room that can be easily disinfected.

Giving a pill

• Place your left hand over the dog's muzzle and raise its head slightly, pressing its jaws gently with your thumb and index finger. Put your thumb into the space behind the long canine tooth and press gently on the roof of the mouth, so that the dog keeps its mouth open. With the right hand, place the pill on the dog's tongue. Close the

dog's mouth, then hold it closed and stroke the dog's throat to encourage it to swallow. If it refuses, hold a tidbit close to its nose. •

Administering eardrops

• Lift the flap of the ear (on long-eared dogs) and use damp cotton wool to clean away any visible dirt or wax, but do not poke around in the ear canal. Tilt the head slightly sideways and hold it still. Put the nozzle of the bottle just inside the ear and administer the correct number of drops. Continue to hold the

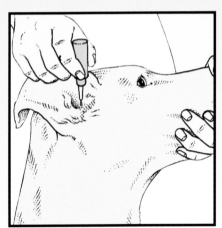

head steady, drop the ear flap and gently massage the ear. Once the drops have penetrated, clean away any excess fluid. •

Applying eyedrops or ointment

• Clean away any discharge from around the eye, then ask a helper to restrain the dog's head. Hold the eye open, bring the hand holding the eye dropper from above and behind, and squeeze in the drops. Hold the dog's head steady for a few seconds so that it does not shake out the drops. Follow the same procedure when applying ointment, then pull down the lower eyelid and squeeze out a small amount of ointment onto the inside of the lid. Hold the eye closed for a few seconds. •

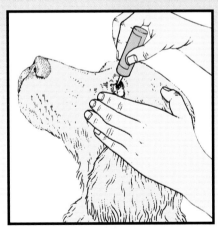

Index

Page numbers in *italic* refer to illustrations